PLEASE DON'T CHANGE THE WORLD

—————◗•●•◖—————

Change the world within

MITYA ORLOV

This book is a fusion of philosophy, Eastern medicine and quantum physics, that all together provide an unusual view on the reflexive need of modern people to change this World. The reader will be taken on a journey of discovery beginning with the factors of health and the significant role played by mindset, to the definition of soul from the perspective of quantum physics and the principles of interacting with the quantum reality, and ultimately arrive at the rules of effective creation of a happy subjective reality within which to live.

Dedicated to all those people
who recognize the real cause of their problems
lies within themselves.

"You must be the change you wish to see in the world."
(Mahatma Gandhi)

CONTENTS

Acknowledgements i

1. Prologue 1

2. Defining Health 3

3. The 6 Levels of Illness Development 7

4. Prepare the Environment for Changes 12

5. Factors of Health 15

6. The Director of Your Life 18

7. Defining the Mind Through Quantum Physics 21

8. Navigating Choices in the Maze of Life 25

9. Hacking Reality 28

10. Asking the Right Questions 31

11. The Principle of Resonance 33

12. Mind vs. Emotions 36

13. Subconscious vs. Conscious 38

14. Mirror Neurons 41

15. Reprogramming the Mindset 44

16. The Principle of Light 47

17. Please Don't Change the World 51

18. The Sun Principle of Free Will 55

19. Epilogue 58

Recommended Literature 61

About the Author 62

ACKNOWLEDGMENTS

I would like to thank my wife - a real inspiration in my life and especially in the process of creation of this book - who is constantly pushing me forward towards new achievements. Thanks to my parents for all their love and support in my life, for the wisdom shared. Love and light to all my family – real treasure of my life.

Thanks to Dr. Konstantin Korotkov who has given me a chance to meet so many outstanding personalities all over the world and opened so many doors in my life. Thanks for sharing knowledge and wisdom.

It was a great pleasure to collaborate with my colleague and friend, Steve Grantowitz, who has helped a lot in proofreading and editing my English in this book. Thanks for the insights and serious attitude – I really appreciate that.

And at the end, I want to thank all my teachers whom I have met in my life, who have shared their knowledge to make it possible for me to share this accumulated knowledge with readers worldwide. This would be impossible without the English teachers throughout my years of education, who have opened for me the door to communication with the whole world.

PROLOGUE

Have you ever tried to assemble a jigsaw puzzle? Using 100 pieces? Using 1000 or even 5000 pieces? Then you know that feeling you get when you have all the needed parts in your hands but don't know how to put them all together. And, to figure this out, you need to spend a lot of time – a precious and limited commodity for most people.

However, assembling a jigsaw puzzle is much easier when you have the overall picture (as provided on the box). Let's imagine that you have 1000 pieces, but you don't have the picture - this is where the real challenge begins - because you are really puzzled.

This scenario doesn't take into account situations when you have more than 5000 pieces, or they are very small or blurred. This is exactly what we all are attempting to do with the vast amount of information presented to us throughout our life.

Imagine that you have all the pieces in your hands,
but you don't know how to assemble them.

This book doesn't pretend to introduce extraordinary and previously unknown information. Rather, most of the topics which will be covered have been known to humankind for some time, and some of it for ages.

The goal of this text is to assist you with assembling the pieces of information you may already be aware of but don't realize how to interconnect to form the bigger picture.

So, together, let's assemble the puzzle.

DEFINING HEALTH

We all want to be healthy, but do we know what health is?

I have decided to start from the beginning - definitions of health. What is grabbing our attention, most of all, in our daily life? Problems. Different types of problems. And, which of these types do we tend to care about the most? Health.

Depending on the state of our health, we can afford to do what we choose to do, attain our goals, and fulfil our plans. It is the fuel that keeps us running.

It has been said, "Health is something that we notice only when we are lacking it." But, the question remains, "What is health?"

Usually, I hear many answers in the form of definitions, but most of them can be reduced to two variants.

"Health is absence of illness" and "World Health Organization definition."

Have you ever thought about the definition of health?

I like the first one, but when I ask the logical follow-up question, "What is illness?", people answer, "Absence of health." This presents a closed loop... and in the end, zero information. Is there an answer through which I can determine the presence of illness at a very early stage, myself, without the consultation of a doctor?

The second variant reads like this: "Health is a state of complete physical, mental and social well-being and not merely the absence of disease or infirmity." Hence, it would seem I need to consult a psychologist, physiologist, and other specialists to determine my health status. I suspect that if I visit several psychologists I will receive several differing conclusions about the state of my psychological health.

I am not saying the W.H.O definition is unacceptable. I do like the specified areas which require our attention to maintain complete health. However, I want to make it simple. Simple for everyone - measurable without the consultation of any doctor, and as objective as possible.

*Are you able to measure your health status
without consulting a doctor?*

There is one definition I prefer over all others. Its origin is in Eastern medicine. I do not know the exact source, and have heard it stated only once from a medical doctor located in a research institute where I was working at the time. The citation is not as important as the principle it relies upon.

It sounds like this: "Health is when you go to the toilet to defecate once a day between 6 and 9 am, the result is of a light brown color with average density and smells like a fresh bakery."

Funny definition, isn't it? But it is based on a very deep understanding of how our "body" works, plus it brings measurability to the definition of health.

You do not need to consult a doctor or invite anyone else to perform an assessment each morning in order to monitor your state. You become your own doctor. A lifetime experiment. I will explain in the following chapters the principles that underlie this definition and why I put "body" in quotes.

THE 6 LEVELS
OF ILLNESS DEVELOPMENT

The interconnection of mental, energetic and physiological levels.
From philosophy to allopathic medicine.

According to the most ancient medical system known to mankind – Ayurveda – each illness passes through 6 stages of development. I will describe each of them briefly, and in a way that is accessible to all readers. We will start with Level 6 as this is the stage during which most people reach out to their health care providers.

This Level is aptly titled **Terminal State**, as it is the last one. This is the time to begin taking antibiotics, or worse, to perform invasive surgical operations. People with a strong nervous system visit the doctor at this point – when they can no longer stand the pain. I will not spend more time discussing this stage as there isn't much to say – it is too late to take any precautions.

The 5th Level is **Symptomatic**. It is the time when you already have some visibly obvious symptoms that do not require a deep medical analysis to recognize there is a problem. People with a sensitive nervous system, and conscious enough to understand that ignoring the symptoms may lead to Level 6, choose to visit the doctor at this time.

Much of modern allopathic medicine is focused on working with people during these last two Levels of illness development. The protocol at this point is temporarily neutralizing the symptoms or performing surgery. Allopathic medicine is not designed to make you healthy, it is designed to keep you semi-healthy so that you will continue to return for consultations and pills. Nothing personal – it's only business.

There were times when family doctors were paid only when everyone in the family was healthy, so they were highly motivated to prevent disease. This is generally not the case anymore.

Integrative and allopathic medicine can help you,
but at different stages of illness.

Let's go further - what leads people to the 5th Level?

It is important to note that all 6 Levels are logically connected. If you are not taking steps to improve your state at a particular Level, then you will eventually progress to the next Level. For example, if in some part of your body there is an **accumulation of toxins** (4th Level), symptoms will appear (5th Level).

A gradual increase of toxins is due to metabolic processes (energy exchanges) that are unable to complete their cycles - a chemical reaction that stops midway causing a portion of the chemicals to not be dissipated enough to be consumed by your organism.

The cause of the accumulation of these toxins? **Metabolic imbalances** (3rd Level) - which may also be described as "incorrect energy flows". There are several types of "energy flows" in our body. Intercellular communication is one of them. Blood and lymph flow is also an example of energy transfer at the material level. Nervous system activity is a flow of electromagnetic signals. Connective tissue transfers electromagnetic signals, too. Chi (or Qi) energy meridians can be added to the list as well. Therefore, if some of the energy is not flowing correctly, it leads to incomplete metabolic reactions, which in turn lead to the accumulation of toxins.

Most integrative clinics and practitioners work with patients on and between Levels 3 and 4: they balance/correct your energy flows (3rd Level) and cleanse/detoxify your body (4th Level). They are more focused on preventing you from advancing to the symptomatic (5th) and terminal (6th) Levels.

This leads us to the root causes of incorrect energy flows and metabolic imbalances which very few specialists today tend to consider.

Incorrect interaction with the world - Level 2. This is one of the hardest Levels to understand, but let's focus on the basic premise. I'm talking about any interactions that you have in your life. It is your attitude towards: environment, animals, your family, your friends, etc., and especially, yourself. If your attitude is imbalanced in one way or another, it will create disturbances in the energy flows in your body.

Eastern and Ayurvedic medicine have a deep understanding of interconnection between the energy flows in your physical body, psycho-emotional state, and your interaction with the world.

Level 1 is the reason for your imbalanced interaction with the world. It is **the set of rules by which you live and interact with your life** – your inner constitution. If you were a computer, it would be your "Operating System" (OS). Or, if you are religious, it may be your Bible, Quran, Torah, or the equivalent. This is your mindset. Your traits and habits.

Think about programs written in your "Operating System".

Some psychologists and life coaches work at this Level. They can help you to define the subconscious programs that are creating problems in your life. But there are few such specialists as compared to the majority of practitioners working between Levels 3 and 6.

So, we may summarize that Levels 1 & 2 are mental, 3 & 4 are energetic/functional, and 5 & 6 are physiological.

Do you remember the funny definition of health from the previous chapter?

If we take into consideration the 6 Levels approach we can understand that this funny definition embraces all of them. All that you experience on mental, energetic and physiological levels during the day will affect the result that you will contemplate the next morning in the toilet.

Your thoughts are affecting the emotions you experience. Emotions are connected to the chemical processes activated or blocked in your body. Your attitude to nutrition and lifestyle will also contribute to the brown result in the toilet next day.

Now this definition of health is becoming deeper and not necessarily as funny.

The root cause of health issues lies in your mindset – the subconscious programs running your OS, also known as habits.

Habits can be changed, willingly. The question is, where do you start?

PREPARING THE ENVIRONMENT
FOR CHANGES

Efficiency of the changes that you apply depends on how well your environment is prepared.

If I were to ask someone to choose which of the 6 Levels would be the appropriate starting point from which to begin treatment, most people would say it is best to start from Level 1 as it is the core of all health problems. I propose a different perspective.

Imagine you are a mayor of a city. The roads in your city are awful, and most of the cars are in poor condition as well. One day you decide to change this situation by buying new cars for all the citizens in your city - hoping they will like this action and it will drastically enhance your reputation.

Great! Everybody exchanges their old car for a new one. What happens next? Well, all the cars will become damaged quickly due to the poor state of the roads - because the environment (roads in the city) was not ready for the changes you wanted to apply.

The environment should fit the changes that you want to apply.

Instead, if you start with repairing all the roads, then the efficiency of your reforms will much higher.

Every chemical reaction has specific border conditions in which it can take place. The same approach can be applied to all living beings – they can live in specific conditions.

This means that if conditions are unsuitable, then chemical reaction will not take place at all.

Most bacteria can survive in an alkaline or neutral pH environment, but will die in an acidic environment. If you want to get rid of specific bacteria, change the environment in which it lives.

For example, fish can live in water with a pH level of 4 to 9. And some of them only between 6 and 9. If the pH goes beyond this limit, all the fish will die.

Your environment should be ready for the intended changes to enable them to be effective and useful.

If we apply this principle to health, I would rather start from Level 4. I would detoxify my body to cleanse it as much as possible. I would stop eating junk food and drinking rubbish drinks. Then, I would balance the energy flows by seeking the services of a massage therapist, or a reiki master, an acupuncturist, and possibly other types of specialists.

Then, my body will be more prepared to accept the changes that I want to bring into my life. Reprogramming will be more effective.

Principle: before doing any reforms in your life, prepare the environment.

Note: I am not saying you need to prepare a perfect or ideal environment to begin applying changes in your life. It needs only to be suitable. Don't get lost in the preparation waiting for the proper moment to start.

FACTORS OF HEALTH

We can change it all: lifestyle, environment, medicine, genome.
Everything is in our hands.

Let's look at our health from another perspective. The World Health Organization provides the main factors which affect our health:

- 45-55% - lifestyle;

- 15-20% - environmental conditions;

- 15-20% - medical system;

- 10% - genome (DNA).

Which factors are in our control?

We can change the lifestyle by preparing the inner environment and reprogramming habits. Many books are devoted to these topics (nutrition, time management, exercise…).

We can be more conscious of the environment in which we live and work and, if needed, we can alter it or move to another place. More and more people are getting involved in the ecological movement.

Well, we likely cannot change the medical system where we live, but we can move to a different location if necessary.

Most people would argue it is impossible to change your DNA, but this is not true. Epigenetics proves it is possible to some degree.

Your DNA is a big library.

Imagine your DNA is an enormous library with many, many rooms. Some doors are open, and some are closed. When a situation occurs in your life, you approach one of the rooms to retrieve its information. If the door is open, you will receive the information and apply it to the current situation. But if the door is closed, you will need to improvise.

What is interesting here is the fact that you can open and close the doors in your DNA library. Such processes are called methylation and acetylation.

One blocks the consequence of some amino acids in the DNA (closing the doors), while the other is activating them (opening the doors).

This means we are able to change our DNA. We can reprogram it. We can control all 4 factors on which our health depends. But who is opening and closing the doors in the DNA library? Who is the key master?

THE DIRECTOR OF YOUR LIFE

*Mind: consciousness and subconsciousness
are our keys to life.*

Usually, when somebody asks where is the general processor or commander within our body we point to our head. Some people point to their heart.

If you ask what is there in your head that is controlling the body and your life, answers will vary. Some people may say the mind, others will say consciousness, and some will say soul. We will try to break down these concepts in the following chapters.

We have come to understand that our mindset is the key master. Remember the Ayurvedic 6 Levels of Illness – it also places mindset at the top.

It doesn't matter which system you prefer – ancient Ayurveda or the modern WHO approach. Either way, you will arrive at the conclusion that our mind, or mindset, is the director of our life.

It can even open and close the doors in your DNA library and reprogram your body.

Before we come to the topic of reprogramming our mindset, let's try to clarify the definitions.

You may be familiar with words such as consciousness and subconsciousness. But what is the difference between them? One can assume they are just two different sections of our mind. So, the mind consists of consciousness and subconsciousness?

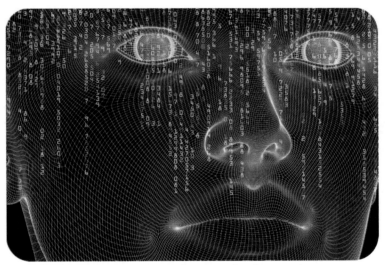

*Consciousness is an editor and subconsciousness
is a set of background programs.*

Both are processing information.

Subconsciousness processes information in an automatic way – like the OS on your computer runs automatic programs in the background without asking the user. These subprograms are crucial for sustaining the life of the organism, or the work of the computer. By default, they are not dependent on the user of the computer or the user of the human body/mind. But if you know how they are made, you can reprogram them and make some corrections. It is in this same way your subprograms can be altered if needed.

Conscious processes are not automatic – they are dependent on the user. Like the user of the computer can open programs, create/edit/delete files, etc., the user of the human body can do the same.

Here comes the confusion. If we put the words subconsciousness and consciousness on the same level, then who is the user that is able to reprogram the mindset at the subconscious level? On which level is the user?

Does consciousness belong to the body level? Or is it on a higher level? Difficult to understand, really. On which level is the body? On which level is the conscious mind? The subconscious mind? And who is that strange user that is able to reprogram the mind?

Let's try to make it clear through the lens of quantum physics.

DEFINING THE MIND
THROUGH QUANTUM PHYSICS

Body, mind, consciousness and subconsciousness. Who is who?

To put everything in the proper order we will need to use some approaches found in quantum physics. Do not be afraid of quantum physics – I will make it simple.

Maybe you have heard of Schrodinger's Cat? It was a hypothetical physics experiment and will be our introduction to the world of quantum physics.

The main concept of the experiment is as follows. Imagine you have an absolutely black box with an incredible level of sound and light isolation preventing you from knowing what happens inside. To begin, you put a cat inside the box. Then you add a nuclear isotope that can dissipate after some time. When it dissipates, it emits some radiation. Then you add a special sensor that can sense this radiation, and you connect a capsule with poisonous gas to this sensor.

With all the components inside the box, you close it, and the magic begins! When the sensor registers the irradiation from the nuclear isotope, which we will assume has a maximum dissipation time of 10 minutes, it opens the capsule and the poisonous gas spreads throughout the inside of the box, and of course the cat dies from this gas.

With the box being closed we don't know if the isotope has already dissipated or not. We can only apply equations to calculate the probabilities.

In quantum physics, everything is described by probabilities. We have two probabilities in our experiment. One – the cat is still alive and the isotope has not yet dissipated. Two –the isotope has dissipated and the cat is dead.

From the point of view of quantum physics, such a closed system is described by the equation:

$$F(a,b,c...) = p1(a,b,c...) + p2(a,b,c...)$$

F – state of the system (box with all the components in it)

a,b,c... – states of each component in the system.

p1 – probability of the first variant – cat is alive.

p2 – probability of the second variant – cat is dead.

You can see that from the point of view of quantum physics the state of the system (F) is represented by the sum of all probabilities. Keep that in mind as we proceed.

For example, 3 minutes after closing the box we will have a 70% probability p1 and 30% p2. After 5 minutes, 50/50, and after 7 minutes, 30% p1 and 70% p2.

This means that if we conduct this experiment 100 times, and open the box after 7 minutes each time, in 70 cases the cat will be dead and in 30 cases it will be still alive.

Here is the important part: what can you see when you open the box? Can you see p1 + p2? No. You can see only p1 or p2. This means you are not able to see both variants at the same time in each experiment.

If you open the box and see the result is p1, what is happening with p2? Why does it disappear from your equation? Do you delete it just by opening the box?

Let's visualize it like this. Opening the box is like entering one door. Let's assume that we have 10 doors. When you enter one of the doors you get one of the probabilities. At the moment you close the box with the cat and all the stuff inside, behind all 10 doors the cat is still alive so it doesn't matter which door you enter – you will face probability p1. After 3 minutes, behind 3 doors the cat will be dead and behind 7 it will be still alive. And so on.

Selecting subjective reality from the
eternal variety in the quantum reality.

Each door represents an alternative reality. When you choose one of these 10 doors/realities what happens to the other 9? Do they disappear? From the point of view of the law of conservation of energy it is impossible. Nothing should happen to them due to the fact we have chosen 1 door and not another. Therefore, we are not destroying other alternative realities by selecting one of them.

Another very important conclusion can be derived from this experiment: we can face only one of the realities or probabilities. Only by repeating the experiment can we see the different variants. But in one experiment and measurement we can see only one probability. It means that a human being is not able to see all the alternative realities at one time. We simplify the quantum reality.

From these facts, we can derive a definition of consciousness. Being conscious means – simplifying the quantum reality. Being conscious is the process of choosing one reality from the infinite set in quantum reality.

So, maybe we are not changing the quantum reality? Maybe we are simply making choices of the subjective reality that we want to enter?

NAVIGATING CHOICES
IN THE MAZE OF LIFE

Main principle of walking in the maze is
making only "right" turns

Imagine that quantum reality is an eternal maze (labyrinth). In order to make it easier for our minds let's make it a regular maze on a 2D surface with very high walls which cannot be climbed and are not transparent. Everything is already pre-designed in it. This means past, present and future states are already imprinted somehow, and you are walking in this maze within your physical body. At any given moment in time you can only be in one location in this maze.

Close your eyes and imagine how you are walking in this maze: making right and left turns, stopping at some intersections.

All our lives are in this journey through the maze and making decisions where to turn next.

This is your life: walking in the eternal maze.

If you have a goal in your life you need to reach a specific point in this maze. Some goals are easy to achieve – you know the way in the maze. If the goal is really great, unusual and located far away from the place (situation) where you are now, you need additional information, guides or hints. You need help. Where can you get it?

One of the first options that comes to your mind is to ask for assistance from someone else. This way works in cases when somebody has already been in a similar place/situation. But bear in mind that the other person's directions will not work 100% in your case where you may have a concrete wall in some locations while the other person may have an opening in their maze. Doors which are open for one person may be closed for another.

How good are you at walking in the maze? It depends on your skill of making choices and facing the outcomes.

When you think you have made a wrong choice, there is nobody to blame. Nobody can really force you to turn in a direction in which you don't

want to go, but… we know that we frequently make such "wrong decisions" under the influence of other people, forgetting that our maze doesn't coincide with their maze. When you made a "wrong" choice it meant that you did not have enough information prior to making the choice.

So, one of the main skills in our life is the skill of making correct choices.

Is there a way of mastering this skill?

Is there a way of hacking the subjective reality in which we live?

HACKING REALITY

Who can help you to get information from the quantum reality? Definition of your soul.

Let's imagine you are going to a new place in the maze of life. Nobody has been there before, and you have not previously had the same situation in your life. What would you do? You will try to collect as much information as possible. It's like solving a hard mathematical problem.

There should be some type of a shortcut. Don't you think so? Some trick? Let's hack this reality!

Now close your eyes and imagine that some part of you is flying above the maze and looking around. This part is trying to find a way to the place you need to go.

It is finding answers to your questions in the quantum reality, while your body is still in the maze.

There is a way to hack the subjective reality,
if you can fly above the maze of life.

Then, this part of you returns back to your body and shares the newfound knowledge, information about the path leading to the desired place in the maze of life. And, suddenly, you know where to go. Suddenly, you have the answer to the question which was bothering you for such a long time.

There are different names for this process: inspiration, intuition, 6th sense, foreseeing, clairvoyance, insight and others.

It may be called different names, but the principle stays the same. You received an answer to your question, from somewhere.

What will you call this part of you that is able to connect to the quantum reality — able to fly above the maze and look around?

From my perspective, these words are describing the process of obtaining information from the quantum reality.

I propose we call this part of us a soul.

The Soul is the part of us that has the capability of extracting information from the quantum reality - to help choose the correct way, the correct answer from multiple incorrect options.

Remember, you are not limited to your subjective reality and this material world! You have a part of you that is able to interact with the eternal database of information (quantum reality) — your soul.

But is it so easy to interact with your soul? Is it so easy to understand the information it is trying to share with you when it returns from its journey in the ocean of quantum reality?

Can just anyone create something by obtaining new information from the quantum reality, or must someone have specific properties or skills to do that?

Let's try to find the answers to these questions, too.

ASKING THE RIGHT QUESTIONS

More accurate the question – more useful the answer.

To obtain an answer from quantum reality you need first to ask a question. If you don't have a question, you will not understand the answer, even if you stumble upon it.

You are aware of a network of computers which embrace the entire planet – the Internet. There is an abundance of information on the Internet. We can assume that quantum reality is just like Internet. You may find there an answer to almost any question. But… some rules and restrictions apply. Knowing them will make your search much more efficient.

To get an answer on the Internet, you have to ask by typing the question in a search engine (like Google, Yandex, Baidu, Bing, etc.). The information is there. At least some of the words you type in the search line should coincide with the answer. The higher the percentage of matching the words of the question with the words in the answer, the higher the accuracy of the proposed answers.

Enter your question here... **Search**

Hint: Correct question has 50% of an answer.

*Visualize: How to ask a question in order
to get maximum useful answer.*

What does that mean? It means that not every person can access information from the information field, or quantum reality. One should be prepared to use enough information in the question field to not only find the answer, but to understand it as well.

The same thing occurs you when you try to interact with the quantum reality. The Soul may be able to access the information, but your mind will not be able to process and understand it if you are not prepared to do so.

This leads us to one of the main principles of the Universe.

THE PRINCIPLE OF RESONANCE

Nothing can affect you if there is no resonance.

In physics, resonance is a phenomenon in which a vibrating system or external force drives another system to oscillate (flatter) with greater amplitude at a specific preferential frequency. Resonance is a multiplication of the power of irradiation of two sources when their frequencies coincide. Each oscillation has its own frequency (measured in Hertz, Hz). In other words: if frequencies coincide interaction via resonance between them takes place, if frequencies do not coincide – they stay independent. No resonance – no interaction.

In a wider sense, resonance is the interaction of everything in this material world, at the level of oscillation. All material particles are oscillating. Why? Let's start with movement.

Movement requires an object capable of moving, and a force that moves the body. Every body has mass. Mass has inertia. Movement is the result of force. Therefore, every body is trying to keep its position due to inertia, and force is always trying to move it. Due to the opposite phenomena trying to compensate each other - every movement is rhythmic. It means that everything is oscillating.

The following are several examples of the Principle of Resonance.

First, what will happen to you if someone shoots at you with a TeraHertz laser (10^{12} Hz frequency)? Almost nothing, because you do not have anything inside your body that oscillates in this frequency range! The laser beam will go through you, through the planet, and continue its path through space.

Second, have you ever read one book several times? If yes, then you have likely thought that each time you read it you discover something new. It happens due to one reason - you tend to have questions in the back of your mind, and when you read the book you are searching (consciously or subconsciously) for answers to these questions. So, although the book remains the same in time, you derive different conclusions from reading it. Again, resonance.

And, the opposite is true - you will never hear and understand the answers to the questions you don't have.

Third, imagine a big field with trees and bushes, lots of flowers, insects, and animals walking around. Now, imagine that a fly is flying above this field. It can see all the beauty of the nature, but then it suddenly sees a pile of manure left by an animal, and finds it interesting. So, it lands on it and begins its investigation. Then, it finds another pile, etc. Imagine what the fly will think about this field: "This field is full of manure!!! All you could ever want!"

Now, imagine that a bee is flying above the same field. It can see all the beautiful flowers, and the nectar on them. So, it lands on the many flowers, one by one, collecting the nectar. What will the bee think? Maybe, "So many flowers in this field! It is magnificent!"

Big field full of blossoms, untouched by humankind.

Both were flying above the same field, at the same time, but their perspective is entirely different because their minds are tuned to different things: one resonates with manure, the other one with nectar. Have you met these types of people? Human-flies and human-bees?

Our mind works in the same way – we interact with those things in life which our mind is tuned in to. If there is no resonance, there will be no interaction. If there is no interaction, there is no effect. Remember, nothing can influence you without resonance. You can apply this principle to any sphere of life.

MIND VS. EMOTIONS

*We assess all information: automatically from the
subconscious level, and mindfully from the conscious level.
Emotions are the result of such assessment.*

Now we know that the key-master of our lives is our mind which has a specific mindset. We have discussed that we have a helper — our soul — which is able to interact with the information field or quantum reality.

But do we really control our mind? Are we really conscious beings?

What will happen to you if someone curses you with all the bad words that he or she knows? Maybe you will be disappointed. Maybe your mood will be spoiled for a day, or a week. Or, maybe you will remember this for your entire life. Bad words resonate with your personal thoughts, causing a reaction. What will happen if you come to a real yogi and do the same? I think – nothing. Why? Because, he doesn't care what you think about him. Therefore, no resonance will occur.

You come to a real yogi and curse him
with all the curse words that you know.

This means that before you experience emotions you have to assess the information (situation). If the assessment tells you that everything is fine, you will have a positive reaction. If not, then a negative one. If you don't care, there are no emotions.

How is this assessment happening? If you are conscious of this process of judgment, you will control the answer and the resulting emotions you experience. But if your mind is floating elsewhere, then you will have an automatic (subconscious) response according to the OS you are running on (recall the 2nd chapter and the 6 Levels of illness) – your mindset.

Do you think that you make decisions consciously in your life? Or, maybe most of them are made automatically (subconsciously)?

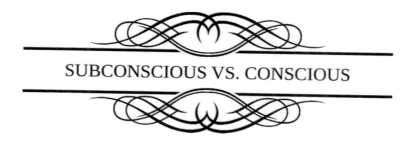

SUBCONSCIOUS VS. CONSCIOUS

Are we really conscious beings?
Or maybe an automatic machine with a little speck of free will?

According to recent findings of scientists, our brain processes around 50 bits per second of information at the conscious level and around 11 million bits per second at the subconscious level.

Correlating results were obtained by scientists while studying human eye movements. Our eyes scan the surrounding space with incredible speed, but most of the information obtained through these movements is not processed consciously. This means that if you ask a person if he/she was looking in specific direction, and he/she answers "no", special eye movement controlling equipment can detect the smallest fluctuations and prove that the eyes were looking in that specific direction. Funny, the owner of the eyes was not aware that he/she was looking in that direction.

There is a variety of scientific research showing that at the subconscious level we are doing much more than at the conscious level. For us, it is not important to calculate the exact ratio of bits processed and movements made at conscious and subconscious levels. Most important is to understand the outcomes of these findings.

We must conclude that we are not conscious beings, but mostly (99.99%) subconscious beings.

This conclusion adds a new level of understanding of the 6 Levels of Illness we discussed earlier. The Mindset (Level 1) is mostly connected to subconsciousness, not consciousness.

What is the relationship between subconsciousness and consciousness?

We can visualize it in several ways.

Focal point of the picture – conscious information, the rest of the picture is subconscious.

Let's imagine that we are photographing a picture with a wide-angle lens. The focus of the camera will be in the center of the captured image and everything will be very clear and precise there. As we move further away from the central focal point the clarity of the image decreases. The focal point is our consciousness and the rest of the image is subconsciousness.

Another example is from the Information Technology sphere. We have already compared our mindset with an operating system (OS). All the subprograms running automatically in the OS represent subconsciousness. But there is a special program (or function) designed specifically for editing the existing code or programs. This Editor is similar to consciousness. You can visualize consciousness as an Editor program or as a user operating the OS from another dimension. The choice is yours.

We have a part of us that has a free will - able to make choices, reprogram/edit the mindset and "create" its own subjective reality.

But are we fully controlling the editing/reprograming process, or is there some type of interference occurring?

MIRROR NEURONS

*Mirror neurons are automatically programming your mindset. Everything
that you perceive affects and programs you
without asking your permission.*

According to recent scientific research, our brain has a special type of neuron – so-called "mirror" neurons. They are fulfilling the "copy-paste" function in our operating system. Whatever you perceive, they pretend it is happening to you even if you are only observing it happening to another person. They are doing this automatically without your initiative.

In one experiment, a group of people passed an initial test of throwing a basketball into a basket. Based on the results, they were divided into two groups such that the average result of each group was equal. Then, for a week, one group practiced playing basketball every day for a couple of hours, while the other group watched the best NBA games on a television for the same amount of time. That second group did not touch a ball even once during the experiment.

After one week, they were tested again. Which group demonstrated better results? The group that practiced? No! The second group. But why?

While the second group was watching NBA games, mirror neurons of the observers were pretending that it was the observer playing the games. So, they were copying movements from the best basketball players in the world. Mirror neurons made it possible to learn how to play basketball without touching a ball. Miracle!

This means that for mirror neurons there is no "I". They do not see any difference between you doing something and any other person doing it. Anything that you see is being automatically copied by mirror neurons. Proof that we are interconnected by nature.

Turn your head maximum left. Visualize that you are turning your head left and stretching all the connected muscles without actual movement. Turn your head again, and the angle should increase.

Try it for yourself. Can you feel happy at a funeral when tens of people are mourning around you? It is almost impossible. Your mirror neurons will not allow you to do that. Instead, they will copy the emotions of the people around you and you will start to grieve as well.

Beside the fact that we are mostly subconscious (automatic) beings, we are also not fully belonging to ourselves. Part of us does not recognize the difference between our "I" and other people around us. Can you imagine how few the number of things we are really able to control in our lives?

How can we gain control over this automatic "copy-paste" functionality of mirror neurons? We should be very careful when selecting the environment in which we live and work - including the people that surround us (friends, coworkers, etc.).

So, if you want to increase the level of your consciousness and control more aspects of your life, you should consider revising the people and environment(s) with which you interact.

REPROGRAMMING THE MINDSET

The keys to being happy and healthy lies in the power of our mindset. Its programming is our main priority.

We have come to understand that to live happily and healthfully we need to take care of our mindset, which defines how we react to events in our daily life. Most of it lies at the subconscious level and determines our automatic responses to these events. We have two main goals: increase the percentage of conscious reactions to events, and reprogram the subconscious responses.

As automatic responses comprise the majority of our reactions, we need to find a way to alter them for the better. And, what are these automatic interactions? They are our habits.

Changing our habits will alter the automatic responses. So, we need to complete several steps to achieve this goal.

Imagine you are writing your life story.

1. You need to decide and define what is "GOOD" and what is "BAD" in your subjective reality. These definitions are your rules to live by. The choices are entirely up to you, however...

Remember the Principle of Resonance. If you decide that being dishonest to others is "good" in your reality, you should be ready for people to be dishonest to you.

2. According to your rules you can surround yourself with "GOOD" people in a "GOOD" environment, and evade the "BAD" options for both.

3. Select "GOOD" habits that you want to possess and you will program them into your subconscious mind - your OS.

4. Start integrating them one-by-one into your life according to their priority.

Some of the habits and traits may take you only couple of months to integrate into your life, while others may take years.

You may try to get rid of the "BAD" traits and habits, but I do not recommend doing this, and I will explain why.

THE PRINCIPLE OF LIGHT

Rather than fight your weaknesses — strengthen your talents.

Now that we know we should reprogram ourselves to make our life happier and healthier, what should we concentrate on?

Whenever we think of self-development, in most cases we think about fighting with our weaknesses or bad character traits. Some people also work on positive traits.

There are very popular quotes that describe this approach. One of them is, "You are your own greatest enemy". And, by following this approach, you constantly struggle with yourself - and your life feels like a never-ending fight.

Let's try to think about this process from a different perspective. And, to do that we will need to answer a couple of questions.

"Does light exist in the physical universe?" I think most of us would answer yes.

Next question, "Does darkness exist?" Most of us would, again, answer yes. But...

We know there is a source of light and it is being emitted in quantums (small portions). So, the quantum of light makes the light "exist".

"Is there a source of darkness?" Possessing a Masters degree in Technical Physics, I've never heard anything about a quantum of darkness. So, from a physical standpoint, darkness doesn't exist.

This means that only light exists.

People label everything in this world. We need to describe everything in words to be able to exchange our thoughts with other people. But sometimes we forget the real meaning of a word.

The word "darkness" describes a place (if we speak about space) with a low amount of light, not a high amount of darkness. Nothing else. There is no source of darkness.

Whenever we see darkness we need to remember that this is a relative term. We call a place "dark" if there is not enough light.

This means we need only to concentrate on the light. Simply increase the power of the light source, and there will be no need to fight with the "darkness".

Yes, it may seem like I'm playing with the words, but, "the way we think is the way we live".

If we are concentrating on the darkness and finding the ways to fight it, our mind and consciousness are focused on something that doesn't exist. Do not tilt at windmills like Don Quixote. It is not effective. Do not waste your energy by trying to fill a cup that has no bottom.

The same principle should be applied when we are thinking of changing something in our life. There is no need to concentrate on the negative points or places — it is not effective. Do not fight with something that doesn't exist. Find the "light source" and work on its characteristics — increase the power of the light.

Imagine that you are fighting with a non-existent enemy.

If you are aware of your weaknesses, or specific negative traits, find your strengths or positive traits that will compensate the weaknesses - and only concentrate on those.

When you start to apply this principle in your life you will see that negative traits don't exist — they were created by your mind to describe a lack of the corresponding positive trait.

In other words, increase your inner light and the darkness will disappear. From this perspective, our life will never be a constant fight. It will transform into an eternal interaction with the light — strengthening our talents.

I call this "real positive thinking".

Each time you think there is something to fight with in your life, remember this principle of the light.

If anything bad appears in your life, it is due to resonance. Do you remember this Principle? Resonance attracts bad things to your life due to a low quality or amount of light emission, not due to "darkness emission" (as it doesn't exist at all).

Stop fighting the windmills — think positive.

PLEASE DON'T CHANGE THE WORLD

*It is so popular today: changing the world
and imprinting your view on others.*

Who wants to change the world?

Whenever I ask this question in a seminar or a conference, people willingly nod their heads or raise their hands to vote for that. But...

I then ask everyone to look around and notice if there are other people in the room who want to change the world. And, they see that almost everyone around them also wants to change the world.

The next question is, "What happens if the way you want to change the world does not coincide with the vision of your neighbor?" This may lead to a minor quarrel, a confrontation, or even a fight.

And, if there is a large group of people wanting to change the world in one way, and another group of people wanting to change the world in another way, war is inevitable. The more people involved in "changing the world", the bigger the conflict.

Please do not change the world. Please.

Do you know the saying, "There is no way to teach others, there is only a way to learn"? If a person doesn't want to learn, you will never be able to teach him/her anything. You can't change anybody in this world, only yourself.

Please do not change the world as the world is quantum reality, and we live only in subjective reality. We are only responsible for our subjective reality, for our own life and health. We are unable to change anything in the quantum reality where everything already exists in all probable variations.

Remember the quote by Mahatma Gandhi? "You must be the change you wish to see in the world."

Listen to your heart and soul when you say to yourself you don't need to change the world... What do you feel? Can you feel some weight of responsibility has fallen from your shoulders? Are you more relaxed and calm?

As soon as you realize that you don't need to change the entire world, or any person other than yourself, you will feel much more relaxed and free. Remember this feeling.

I can foresee that some readers may ask: "So, you mean there is no way to change life on planet Earth?"

Honestly, no. Don't aim for that. You can change your life on planet Earth, and exemplify the way you want it to be overall. But, remember that other people on this planet have their own free will and need to make their own choices. If some people want to follow you, they will; if some do not, they won't - and you cannot force them to do so.

I'm not saying you don't have to do anything to change your life and/or environment. Or that you don't have to help other people around you. Help others only if they need it, or if you are ready to face the consequences of your actions if the person has not asked for your assistance. Sometimes people do not express gratitude when you help them, even if they asked for help. Be ready for that, too.

This is a multiplayer reality that fits everybody's needs:
conscious and subconscious.

If you have legitimate power, given by others, then you might feel that you can change the world. The truth is, you can only change the scenery in which people live, but you can't change the subjective reality of any person if he/she doesn't want it changed.

You want to feed homeless dogs? Go for it! Do not assume you will be able to help all homeless dogs in the world. You are only one player in this multiplayer game. Make your choice and get rid of the obligation to change the world.

I know it is hard to simplify this principle, but from the perspective of quantum physics, you are not able to change the quantum reality – you can only choose your own subjective reality.

What if the world is designed such that souls must learn their own lessons by passing through difficulties? What if our souls are here specifically to do that? What would you say to someone who would not let you pass your lesson - who interrupts your learning process? "Help"? Will you become angry or disappointed? Exactly!

Let others pass their own lessons.

Remember that some of the lessons can be passed only in groups. This means that there is nothing wrong with passing some lessons together with others, but only if they agree to do that. Remember free will.

So, make your own choices and change your own subjective reality - your life. That's it.

THE SUN PRINCIPLE OF FREE WILL

Do not interrupt others' lives. If you were not asked – do not answer. If you have interrupted – be ready for any reaction.

Raise your head during a sunny day and look at the Sun in the sky. Do you think the Sun really cares how many people are walking under its light? Most likely, no. It just emits the light. It just fulfills its function.

Let's imagine the Sun is conscious.

What would happen if the Sun tries to deliver light to every living being whenever it wants to do so?

In some cases, it will be considered "good". But certainly, there will be cases when it will be considered to be "bad". Do you agree?

Maybe you are trying to sleep and you don't need the sunlight.

Maybe you have applied a citrus essential oil to your skin and it is dangerous to be in direct sunlight.

Maybe your eyes become irritated when there is too much sunlight.

Maybe you want to watch the beautiful stars in the night sky. And so on.

In all of these cases, sunlight will not be welcomed, and will be treated as a "bad" thing.

This means the Sun should respect your free will and allow you time or space to avoid it.

Imagine the Sun is chasing you and you have nowhere to hide.

Now, imagine that you are a source of light, or a source of information.

Case 1. You care about how many people with whom you are sharing the light or information. So, your aim in life is to share the light/information with the maximum number of people.

Then, you will try to reach people in any place and at any time. You will likely forget to ask them if they need your light/information. And, most likely, you will just irritate those people. You will start using phrases such as, "You have to listen to this...". You will insist others listen to your information or receive your light. And if people refuse, it may irritate you, or you may become disappointed.

Each time someone rejects your light/information you will see it as not fulfilling your aim in life and it will lead to sadness and grief, or even depression. It will be a constant fight. You will be dependent on the external world and others' opinions.

Case 2. You do not care about how many people have your light/information. You care about its quality. You care about how easily it is understood by other people - so you master your skills in sharing it and work on increasing the amount you can share. You respect the free will of other people. If they are not receiving your light/information, they are not irritated, and you are not disappointed, because there are only two causes: they are not ready for it, or you have not delivered it in a way appropriate for each specific person. No fight for new "clients" or "disciples".

Which case do you prefer?

Should you approach everyone to deliver your light or share your information if you were not asked for it? Respect the free will of each person, of the world outside.

Do you like to help people? Are they always happy when you help them? Most likely you can remember cases when you have received a negative reaction to your "help". Why does it happen?

EPILOGUE

Do not impose, just propose.
How to live a happy and healthy life.

In every country, throughout different centuries, and in every culture, there are personalities that have influenced the world on a large scale - and we are used to claiming, "they changed the world". Do you want to add some change to the world, too?

If we look closer into each of these cases we will find proofs of the principles listed in this book. Such personalities were proposing another view of the world (quantum reality), and their view resonated with the minds of other people. The more connections they had, the more people were involved in the resonance effect.

And, they were not imposing their view on the world or on other people - they were proposing.

Proposing is a much less aggressive way of interacting with the quantum reality. It takes into account the "Sun Principle of Free Will", the "Principle of Light" and the "Principle of Resonance", too. It leaves a space for others to make their own decisions regarding the proposed view.

When you are imposing your view on the quantum reality and other people, you are not following these principles. So, you must be prepared for the outcomes of such behavior and the reaction of the environment and surrounding people. In many cases, as we have discussed earlier in this book, you will receive a negative answer (for you) from the external world when you try to impose your view.

Real leadership is to attract people
by providing resonant information.

Do not impose, just propose.

Master the skill of making your own choices and change your persona subjective reality.

Remember that only by correcting and reprogramming your mindset as discussed earlier in this book, will you be altering your interaction with the world that has all the built-in possibilities. Only this attitude will really lead you to the happy and healthy life in this maze of quantum reality, and create a proper subjective reality that will specifically suit your needs.

RECOMMENDED BOOKS

1. Michael Newton (1994). Journey of Souls: Case studies of Life between Lives.

2. Dawson Church (2009). The Genie in Your Genes: Epigenetic Medicine and the New Biology of Intention.

3. Rami Bleckt (2012). The Forgotten Canons of Health and Harmony.

4. Eckhart Tolle (1999). The Power of Now: A Guide to Spiritual Enlightenment.

ABOUT THE AUTHOR

Dmitry V. Orlov received his Master of Sciences in Technical Physics from the Saint-Petersburg State Technical University of Information Technologies, Mechanics and Optics – Department of Laser Technologies. He is currently General Manager at Bio-Well Company, which produces the Bio-Well device and its software. Mr. Orlov is also the Founder and General Director of AVD Company – focused on the studies of human ecology and living space ecology (geopathic stress analysis) and their interconnection.

Mr. Orlov is the author of more than 20 papers published in various journals and international conferences thesis, and 7 author tutorials written on the subject of Electro-Photonic Imaging/Gas Discharge Visualization.

He is the recipient of multiple research grants and awards, and actively conducts seminars worldwide on EPI/GDV while furthering the development of the Bio-Well system - a new era of integration of Western and Eastern approaches to the human body and health assessment.

Contact: mityaorlov@gmail.com